GRIMOIRE

GRIMOIRE

New Scottish Folk Tales

Robin Robertson

with drawings by
Tim Robertson

PICADOR

First published 2020 by Picador
an imprint of Pan Macmillan
6 Briset Street, London ECIM 5NR
Associated companies throughout the world
www.panmacmillan.com

ISBN 978-1-5290-5111-7

Printed and bound by CPI Group (UK) Ltd, Croydon, CR0 4YY

Visit **www.picador.com** to read more about all our books
and to buy them. You will also find features, author interviews and
news of any author events, and you can sign up for e-newsletters
so that you're always first to hear about our new releases.

for our sister
Nicola
and in memory
of our father and mother

a pin to see a pappy show
a pin to see a die,
a pin to see a wee man,
running up the sky

Games & Diversions of Argyleshire

CONTENTS

INTRODUCTION

It is no accident that Robin Robertson's *noir* narrative poem *The Long Take* was shortlisted for the 2018 Man Booker Prize for fiction, the first poetic work ever to achieve that distinction. Robertson is a writer who understands the power of story: a binding power that stretches back thousands of years to the time when we tried to make sense of the world by sitting round fires and creating scenarios – myths and superstitions – to explain the inexplicable.

It's also no accident that *Grimoire* is subtitled *New Scottish Folk Tales*. We live in an age of shape-shifting and transformation, constantly wrong-footed by the disjuncture of appearance and reality, and this book is a timely reminder that it was ever thus. Quite often, ancient magic feels as useful a clue to our lives as behavioural science. And there is a long tradition in Scottish storytelling of *doppelgängers*, those eerie second selves: other aspects of our personalities that we'd prefer to keep hidden – until we need their skills in the service of our needs, our desires.

I've long admired Robin Robertson's narrative gift. In short lyric poems and longer works, he employs his extraordinary economy with words to give shape to the story below the surface. One of my favourite examples, 'Law of the Island', is shocking and horrifying in itself, but its sixteen short lines hint at the dark spooling-out of events that led us here. Like so many of the early folk tales, it has at its root a caution – don't be The Other, don't be different; different is dangerous. Obey the rules, or at least *appear* to obey. Be part of the community or be expelled from it.

In this collection of poems – this manual for summoning demons – we are led into a world of magic and mutability, of savagery and dread, of pity without sentimentality. Weather and landscape are agents in the drama: the drama conjured by these words and images, these timeless predicaments, leaving us terrified and exhilarated. Tim Robertson's wonderful drawings feed those weird imaginings, haunting us long after we close the book. As a character says in one poem, 'All I see, now, is everything that's lost.'

And then there's the language. There's no escaping the glorious delight Robin Robertson takes in the various tongues available to him. English, Scots and Gaelic all have their place here, all brought into the service of the precision with which he writes, the uncanny resonance of these new folk tales whose images stick in our heads as if glued in place with drying blood: 'a rack of bones like a sprung trap'.

If you love stories, you will love this book. If you think poetry is for softies, think again.

Val McDermid, 2020

GRIMOIRE

OF MÙTHADH / MUTABILITY

This book is for the taken: for all those feart of the glamour,
the skaith of the evil eye – weird-set, ill-minted
or only wildering – their bodies in motion, flowing
or full-flown, rapt with heart-hunger.

*

Grass twists up through my hair now
and my mouth is full of stones.
Tell my mother and father I am coming, tell them
I have not grown old.

THROUGH THE STRUAN DOOR

There is the story of a boy, fetched from the water.

He was set to work, feeding the cauldron of the she-witch –
a whole year, stirring the herbs that would magic
wisdom and future-sight to her two children,
before he made the mistake.
Licking some spilt juice from his hand, his mind turned;
he knew then what would happen next.
Raging that he'd swallowed the cream
of her enchantment, the glamourie,
the witch went after him.
      Gifted with knowledge now,
           he changed to the ways of a mountain hare
so she made the form of a hunting hound,
           he turned to a mackerel
      slipping under the waves,
so she swam into the shape of a sea-otter bitch,
           he flew up with the wings of a starling
so she stooped from the sky as a hawk,
           and then he knew it was almost done
      so he lost himself in a field, as an ear of corn,
and she made herself back to a huge brown rat and ate him down.

But he did not die. He just set seed, inside. The witch waited,
and nine months later she was ready with her knife.
Re-born, he was so beautiful she couldn't cut his throat –
so she tied him inside a leather-skin bag, dropped it
into a coracle, and sent him out to sea.

But he did not die, and was found alive
on another coast, after weeks on the ocean,
and he grew to become a bard, they say,
singing forever of her greed and cruelty.
How being strong is being many.

*

My doors swing open. In the looking-glass
the hair on the side of my head pricks up,
coarsening, going from red to grey, each ear
twisting outwards into a cup; my chin
lengthens to beard, the forehead nubs
grow heavy, hardening to horn,
a new shape becoming visible;
then the eyes roll back into white
and start to spin like a drum
through all the changes, settling with a soft click
into goat:
each fat, black, horizontal bar of pupil
a floating letter-box.

What have I ushered in now: already
streaming over this threshold?
A body in flux – a man or a beast or a god –
a kind of Christ, perhaps: busy at his endless resurrections.

BY CLACHAN BRIDGE

I remember the girl
with the hare-lip
down by Clachan Bridge,
cutting up fish
to see how they worked;
by morning's end her nails
were black red, her hands
all sequined silver.
She unpuzzled rabbits
to a rickle of bones;
dipped into a dormouse
for the pip of its heart.
She'd open everything,
that girl.
They say they found
wax dolls in her wall,
poppets full of human hair,
but I'd say they're wrong.
What's true is
that the blacksmith's son,
the simpleton,
came down here once
and fathomed her.
Claimed she licked him
clean as a whistle.
I remember the tiny stars
of her hands around her belly
as it grew and grew, and how

after a year, nothing came.
How she said it was still there,
inside her, a stone-baby.
And how I saw her wrists
bangled with scars
and those hands flittering
at her throat,
to the plectrum of bone
she'd hung there.
As to what happened
to the blacksmith's boy,
no one knows
and I'll keep my tongue.
Last thing I heard, the starlings
had started
to mimic her crying,
and she'd found how to fly.

AT ROANE HEAD

You'd know her house by the drawn blinds –
by the cormorants pitched on the boundary wall,
the black crosses of their wings hung out to dry.
You'd tell it by the quicken and the pine that hid it
from the sea and from the brief light of the sun,
and by Aonghas the collie, lying at the door
where he died: a rack of bones like a sprung trap.

A fork of barnacle geese came over, with that slow
squeak of rusty saws. The bitter sea's complaining pull
and roll; a whicker of pigeons, lifting in the wood.

She'd had four sons, I knew that well enough,
and each one wrong. All born blind, they say,
slack-jawed and simple, web-footed,
rickety as sticks. Beautiful faces, I'm told,
though blank as air.
Someone saw them once, outside, hirpling
down to the shore, chittering like rats,
and said they were fine swimmers,
but I would have guessed at that.

Her husband left her: said
they couldn't be his, they were more
fish than human,
said they were beglamoured,
and searched their skin for the showing marks.

For years she tended each difficult flame:
their tight, flickering bodies.
Each night she closed
the scales of their eyes to smoor the fire.

Until he came again,
that last time,
thick with drink, saying
he'd had enough of this,
all this witchery,
and made them stand
in a row by their beds,
twitching. Their hands
flapped; herring-eyes
rolled in their heads.
He went along the line
relaxing them
one after another
with a small knife.

It's said she goes out every night to lay
blankets on the graves to keep them warm.
It would put the heart across you, all that grief.

There was an otter worrying in the leaves, a heron
loping slow over the water when I came
at scraich of day, back to her door.

She'd hung four stones in a necklace, wore
four rings on the hand that led me past the room

with four small candles burning
which she called 'the room of rain'.
Milky smoke poured up from the grate
like a waterfall in reverse
and she said my name
and it was the only thing
and the last thing that she said.

She gave me a skylark's egg in a bed of frost;
gave me twists of my four sons' hair; gave me
her husband's head in a wooden box.
Then she gave me the sealskin, and I put it on.

BESIDE LOCH IFRINN

Late January, and the oak still green,
the lambs in the field, and the blossom blown.
The season miscarried, the whole year
broken before it began, and I'm standing here
where winter should have been:
a reived man, a man forspoken.

A woman's kiss will lift you all morning.
A woman's curse will grave you to hell.

By the wellspring on the high moor I saw the day
change colour:
watched lightning root in the far woods;
the sky blink.
Fire-shocks, then a scour of rain, a skail-wind
nagging in through the mirk, scuddering,
dishing it down, rain
turning to sleet, to hail, to snow.
And then the cold
– which had been waiting –
dropped.
The green heath silvered:
every leaf
singled out like rosemary.
The wellspring went milky as a dead eye,
smoked with ice,
though just as the surface froze I caught sight of it
– a clay doll, a *corp-criadha*, busied with pins –

and I started down for home.
Where far below I saw the loch-water
going from grey to white: its long fetch
shaved by draw-knife, scythe and sickle,
into ice, with the whipped spray turning hard in the air
and splintering on the shore.

The next day, the ice so thick
we cut holes in it so the fish could breathe,
and we gathered round to watch them –
the trout rising – crowding tight
up into a gasp of mouths, silver and pink,
these bright sheaves, alive there in the ice.

Then the cold went down too deep,
and the fish were locked, like till, in the glass.
Birds fell stiff from the sky; every lamb died.
The cows that were left gave more blood than milk.

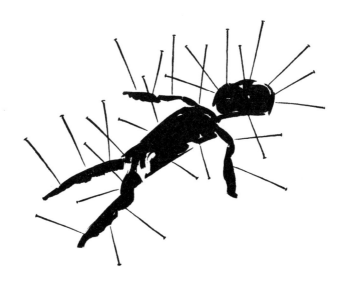

They found young Neil MacLean, the stammerer,
roped to a tree, libbed, with his tongue
shelled out of his head, dressed in red icicles;
Betty Campbell frozen solid in her bath,
forehead scored with the cross. I saw
Macaulay's mare with the bleed on the brain
going round her field faster and faster till she bolted
straight into the stable wall.
I saw a fox
with a firebrand tied to its tail
going over the high cliff, bundled in flames.
And off to the west, a funeral procession
on the side of a hill where no road lay.

Three months under winter; until winter broke.
They tested the loch with their toes:
the blister of air squeezed
white under the ice, wobbling back
like a spirit levelling.
It took their weight for a while,
and they couldn't tell what was ice and what was shore:
till the loch creaked and a mile-long crack appeared
and they watched their footprints soften, sink, dissolve,
their hard and perfect world falling to thaw.

A woman's kiss will lift you all morning.
A woman's curse will grave you to hell.

The thing in the wellspring is gone: the clay
worn away to a bed of pins.
I am taken. I am not right; only barely
in the likeness of a man, walking from Loch Ifrinn
in a pang of birdsong,
carrying myself
on a hill where no road lies.

IN EASGANN WOOD

Rain works the road;
its grey hand passing over and over, in waves: lashing,
stotting down. A stour-wind's in the trees,
churning their heads, and the sky's
full of leaves and the sky is raging:
it will not subside
and will not cease,
and will not be consoled.

As thunder brings the toads, so rain draws worms
from the ground, the rapt god
to this bedroom window – to this house
of panic, of closed mouths,
a bird trapped in every room.
Listen to me. The man who lies beside you:
he's not the man I was, the man I used to be.
I think the wind is easing –
I take that as a sign from the other world
until I remember the other world has abandoned me.
Listen. I will tell you everything. Tell you both.

No birds fly over Coille nan Easgann,
the sacrificial wood; no animals stray there,
only the insects and worms can make use of it.

The first was that daftie, Doogie McRae:
moon-struck, wanting a feather in the wing.
I found him hunkered in the ruined church;

dust round his mouth from eating moths again.
As we reached the wood, the dusk was drawing in,
erasing every tree, and he was pleading,
offering a piece of chalk, a white marble,
a hawk's tail spread like a hand of cards.
I took him to the black burn, under the snags,
and hung him by his feet over the dark water
and fed his face to the eels.

I told Mary Greig about the deer-couch in the wood
where they slept – that I had a half of whisky;
she fell for it all: the flattened bracken,
the fresh fallow droppings like liquorice.
She was full rank by the bottle's end
and I had to disorder her, trying
to get my fingers in her purse, and she wanted it
well enough I could tell, so I riddled her through
and shot my roe – and left her
in her peltry of jellies and syrups
with a smile that went right round her head.

That long cullion, Sandy Gallivaster,
wanted a go at Mary
so I took him to the wood and showed him.
She didn't look so good now; and then
suddenly neither did he, when I smacked him
with a rock and then cut him to collops,
made force-meat of his stupid legs,
hard-gralloched him and glibbed him, and pinned
his stones on a blackthorn bush for remembrance.

They're all still there somewhere, those three,
in Easgann Wood, mulching the trees,
and we have the riddance of them,
but I am done with that. That place is evil.
There: I confessed to you, and to him –
that face in the window. Let's make a peace.
Would you accept this,
this gift of hands, this necklace?
I think you will.

UNDER BEINN RUADHAINN

Three moons in the sky
the night they found him
drowned in Sawtan's Bog;
just his cap, sitting there
and his wee fat hands poking out.

It was no loss to the village,
I told them next morning,
and the villagers agreed.
Horn-daft, he was,
havering and glaikit
and scaring the children.

I mind that time
he picked up a mouse and ate it, quick,
in two mouthfuls;
set the tail aside
on the ground
like a cocktail stick.

I used her well, after that,
his Jennie,
still in her widow's weeds,
jilping into her
whenever I could,
in the barn or the boat-house
or off in the fields.
She slipped two or three out at least,

and sank each one in a lobster creel.

Her head was away
by the end, as mad as her man
and no good to me.
She sleeps now
under Beinn Ruadhainn, her face
covered in ivy,
scab, and sticky-willow.

Then the dreams came.
Last night: the burning loch,
so full of bairns
they bobbed to the surface
with their hair on fire;
black snow; rain
like razorblades;
the foosty-faced man,
there at every corner,
hands furred with grey-mould.
And her, as always,
star-naked, hatching
in the herring-nets.
The last I remember was my body
being driven with sticks through the town
to Sawtan's Brae, and hanged.

I broke from sleep and sat up in the dark.
I groped around for the matches
and the matches were put in my hand.

INSIDE TOBAR NAM MARBH

Four years old, I was, when her thrawn mood finally snapped.
'What you staring at? That daft face on you.
You're always gawking, always *querious*.
Watch the wind doesn't change, or you'll stay like that . . .'
So I stayed and watched the wind so long I became it;
became it, for its very changing.

My sklent eye took in everything –
the fear, the wonder of this world:
the haughland; the simmer dim; that broken bird
like a furtive Christ, moving, in the half-light, tree to tree;
the fox on the beach, the deer at gaze, the bite of fire
at the gorse-field; the way men passed the dead
through a hole they'd made in the wall, then closed it fast
against the soul returning. Snow-wreaths
in the high hills, the low lochs steaming in the dawn;
the way a living girl would take my hand and walk.

At what point do we see that beauty doesn't last, even in memory;
that the happiest days of our lives have already passed?
And now I see too much – *eyes far ben*, as Mother always said –
watching them walking, the ghosts of the dead,
but seeing also the ghosts of the living: each one of them
that's already caught their death. Co-walker,
double-ganger, the *taibhse*, the fetch.
I have the curse and gift: the two sights.

My sister has a drib of it too, but her eye is kinder.

Last year, on her birthday evening – her love
long away on some far ocean – she climbed
above the summer shielings to find
her secret patch of averins, the cloudberries,
to see if they were ripe, to read them for their signs.
Was he still fine and halesome, his skin firm, and sweet?
And as she reached to pull a berry, a knife
fell from the sky and stuck, sair-sunk in the plant.
When her sailor man came home the next spring, he told her
how he'd stood that same night
at the ship's rail, paring an orange,
looking over the side at the ocean, thinking of her.
And in his dwam he dropped it, his favourite knife
with the ivory handle, into the deep.
She went to her pocket and opened a napkin,
and there was the knife that he'd lost.

All I see, now, is everything that's lost.

At the kirk last Sabbath: three gone in one day. Old Jeanie
sitting alone in the family pew: there, but not there.
We looked at each other, but her place was empty.
Iain, the lobsterman, at the back of the chapel, his head
glowing with that flare of sea-light, the waterburn;
jacket dripping, sea-water in those boots
all fankled in a creel, and there, about his mouth,
a string of pearls.
I sat along from Iseabail of the blue eyes, the girl
I'd wearied for all my life, her eyes gone white.
Waiting by her bed for five days after, as the sickness took,

as she died for good;
watching the flesh of her arm dimpling now and then
as if pressed in by fingers, a shadow sometimes
crossing her face, as if someone bent in for a kiss.

Old folk, hollowed out and grey, the baby in the lochan,
the red suicides, the boy with the withered hands.
Every face is the face of a gravestone, spalling away.

I'll drink enough to block it out: be blind.
I go to the looking-glass and see nothing:
just empty space and the other wall, behind.

NEAR GLEANN NAM FIADH

All night preparing: the pelts oiled, blades whetted, the flanes
checked for truth and sharpness, set loose enough
there in the quiver, before the dawn, before the Becoming.
To hunt the stag with honour, Father said, you must
change your shape and nature: assume his form.
Latching on the head-piece, the skull-cap with its horns,
I walked soft into the morning, alert, changed:
no longer man but hart, red deer, *fiadh*, stag.

We'd followed the herd through Làirig Ruadh
where the pass ravined down to Rankil Burn, nosing the deer
deep into the hard cleuch they could never resolve.
The king and his hounds were behind me when the lead buck
turned and roared, clattering forward
up through the rocks, plunging toward the royal colours,
and I stretched out
and took hold of his horns, wrestling him down
on one shoulder, antler to antler.
Waving the royal party to cover, I let the beast go –
off, far beyond the gorge to the high ground
where I struck him fairly,
my arrow singing to the wound.
When I reached him, he could not quite break breath, just
dropped his head, as if in consent.

And I watched as he changed from a god to a human
and back to a deer, ready to be re-made.

After stooping him through with my dirk, they blew the *mort*
for the time of the Breaking.
I opened him, throat to tail, right hoof to left, using bread
to mop the blood, which went in a pocket I'd made in his hide;
cut through the shoulders, sheaved the flesh from the breast;
released the offal, the inmeat, redding it clean in the burn
and then sliving it up in gobbets with the bread in the skin-pouch
till it was all just a guddle: a thick, pink porridge.
Not a crumb of bread or a drop of blood must be lost.
After the debowailling, the fleshing. He smelt
strong and creeshie, this one,
and the dogs drew in hard and were held back
as I unhedded him, and jointed him – shank, shoulder, haunch –
then finally returned him to his hide, all re-assembled, sewn up,
before I lifted his head, with its crown of horns, and set it home.
He would be carried back like that, on a hurdle.
Acorné, sanglant, fracted.
The dogs' reward was the packet of paunch and bloody bread;
the priest and the judge would get the shoulders,
the poor the neck and ribs, the king the rest.

Someone would place the tongue of the deer
on the tongue of the celebrant.
The chine, with its tenderloin meat, was mine.

The king gave me this land after that, in thanks for his life.
But I went searching for bigger beasts, the sixteen-pointers,
tracking further into the mountains, the bog and heather mureland,
till I was forwandered, lost. The deer had gone.

After long in this wilderness, wasting and delirious, head birling,
a girl appeared from nowhere, gesturing me to follow,
and she seemed to swing with that grace I'd forgotten, her feet
leaving slots in the soft ground behind.
Hidden in a belt of trees, her people were gathered,
and I pointed to my mouth and gut and they showed me the burn
that flowed outby, brought me moss and leaves to eat
– the sweetmeats of angels – then, tired to the bone, I slept.
Croaks and bleats. What are the names of my children? My wife?

My own name? I am running now, running with the deer, moving
with them over the hills like cloud-shadows, or fleet-water.
And now I'm awake, and running again. Trying to remember home.

One day I came upon the road to my village. The village was gone.
The stone walls overthrown and blackened, open to the sky,
the grass mound at the end
where they played, where the women dried the washing,
now a sea of crosses.
A man came out of the trees, looking just like Finlay,
but old and doddery, and staring hard.
He said the reivers had come and burnt it all. Gone.
He thought I'd died here too.
'Don't you see?' I said, 'I joined them.
For a week there I was living with the deer.'
'Longer than that, old friend.
You've been gone these twenty years.'
'Ah,' I nodded, 'All gone then. Gone for good,'
stealing a glance at hock and fetlock,
my hard, bright, pretty hooves.

BEYOND THE DUBH-CHLADACH

Seven years we'd waited;
three bairns lost inside, and two born dead.
Rab blamed himself, then me,
then the crone on the next island, then the wee folk –
the *sìthchean* – the fair folk, the peerie folk.
So when I started to show for certain, he went to work:
pulled a handful of nails from the ruined jetty, gathered
pieces of oak and elder and the sacred rowan;
began filling a bucket with stail; laid out
the reaping hook, the Bible, his silver sixpence, the gold ring,
and with his joiner's tools made us a cradle
of the holy wood, and nailed it round with iron.

As my time grew close, he drew water from the well,
collected mussel-shells to hang from the beams with bindweed
so they'd clack above the crib;
mistletoe and the sixpence for the bed, and leaves of the *mòthan*
to spread out under me, as I came to fruit.
There was no minister on these rocks and no saining for me here,
so Rab had a wreath of rowan over the bed, the Bible
held open by the rusted shears that made the shape of the cross,
the bucket of *maistir* there
against the grey folk, the noiseless ones,
and a cup of well-water with the gold ring in it
for the three mouthfuls that would save me.

And saved we were.

He was beautiful, our son: blue-eyed, fair; fresh as meltwater.
I took him out one morning, to the machair, laying him down
on a cushion of clover at the marram's edge
where he tilted his head to hear, like a bird;
watched, as I picked spring flowers – marsh marigolds, vetch,
cowslips, primroses and pansies, dog violets and thrift.

It was a false spring, though, that year;
the cold held on, deep-rooted in the ground.
We walked a lit candle three times round the crib;
washed him three times in saltwater, passed him
three times over the fire,
but saw he was wrong:
always feeding, always famished. Ravenous, thirsty,
he took more than both of us, but never grew.
When I so much as touched him, he cried out –
girning and yowling all day and night, like a snared rabbit.
Rab wouldn't look at him, wouldn't use his name,
called him misgrown; a mimmerkin. Worst of all: *spelled*.
'We must cast the faery out,' he said, rising to his feet.
'Inside their hollow hills – I've heard men tell –
the floors are paved with the teeth of bairns.'

He put him in a foxglove bath, brought in a shovel
heavy with salt, a cross drawn through it,
laid it on the fire to burn.
He would have burnt the child if I'd let him.
'Our boy's been changed, taken away –
this creature left behind, to eat us empty.
It's either trial by fire or water. You decide.'

I carried him down to the beach that evening, the tide coming in
and my heart in flitters. As I laid him down at the sea's lip
there was a rustling sound, like wind in the trees, or a hawk
stooping to the kill,
and I looked over the water to the far skerries
to see a grey-haired man, levering himself up onto a rock.

Is the way he came
the way he's now gone back?

Mother always said that we wear our dreams – all living things:
the goshawk shows on his breast a flock of geese,
the mountain hare becomes snow in winter; the mackerel
carries the streamoury of the north-dancers on its back,
the silver-green and barred black
that ebbs to grey when it's taken from the sea.
So our son had eyes the blue of the far places,
and he wore his skin like water.

For some it's not long, the waiting, for that
decay of light – when all is flown, all faded, washed away.

When I reached the cottage, the crib was still empty.
The crib lies empty still.

BEFORE THE DONNACHAIDH FALLS

I watched a boy left on the cold strand,
I went into the shape of a red stag,
saw two worlds with the two sights
– dreaming my crimes and my punishments –
mad for death in the eel-wood,
witched on the moor to a revenant,
I went to the shape of a seal, a goat,
in the hurt world, at its ragged edge,
where a boy is fetched from the water.

*

I went into the shape of water,
the shape of a wave on the black shore,
moving myself through the blue cauldron
and the faery pools
on the way to the gorge
and the Donnachaidh Falls.

The river in me is black.
I am the god, the beast that leaves no prints,
the pounce of wind on the sea, that place
where the lake darkens
and the surface breaks. I went,
taking the shape of water.

A man, a woman, then I turned to a starling,
mackerel, otter; I made the shape

of a heron, lobster, river-trout, fox,
an eel, a rabbit, a goshawk,
I changed to the shape of a deer
and stayed that way.

I made myself into fire, horned with flame,
I fell like sleet, like a mist of arrows,
rankling arrows, wing to wing;
I fell like forests, cities, whole kingdoms,
I forged myself into the blue blade
that made my wound.

Failing now, I am making a ghost – the long
flume of a ghost – tying all these bird-wings
to my back and arms
and climbing the cliff, right to the roaring top
and I am there, and you can see – see
the Donnachaidh falls.

Notes & Acknowledgements

Versions of almost all these pieces first appeared in the *London Review of Books*. My thanks to Jean McNicol and her colleagues.

'By Clachan Bridge', 'At Roane Head' and 'Under Beinn Ruadhainn' are collected in *Sailing the Forest*.

'At Roane Head' won the 2009 Forward Prize for Best Single Poem.

With thanks to my editor, Don Paterson, my agent, Peter Straus, and to Pàdraig MacAoidh/Peter Mackay for checking the Gaelic.

Karin Altenberg made these poems possible. Tim gave them shape.

'By Clachan Bridge' is for Alasdair Roberts, 'At Roane Head' for John Burnside, 'Beside Loch Ifrinn' for Catherine Lockerbie, 'In Easgann Wood' for Don Paterson, 'Under Beinn Ruadhainn' for Andrew O'Hagan, 'Inside Tobar nam Marbh' for Maggie Fergusson, 'Near Gleann nam Fiadh' for Richard Scott, 'Beyond the Dubh-Chladach' for Duncan McLean.

Of Mùthadh/Mutability

(a protection spell)

mùthadh: (Gaelic) change, mutability, metamorphosis; pronounced '*moo*-huh'

glamour: magic, enchantment (cf. glamourie, gramarye, grimoire) *skaith*: hurt, harm, damage

weird-set: fated, destined, cursed

ill-minted: malformed

wildering: going astray, bewildered, lost

flowing: unstable, changeable

heart-hunger: a longing for affection

Through the Struan Door

Struan: anglicisation of *srùthán* (Gaelic) meaning 'place of streams'

story of a boy: a version of the Welsh legend of Taliesin

By Clachan Bridge

clachan: (Gaelic) hamlet or small village

rickle: pile, heap

stone-baby: the medical term is *lithopedion*; this occurs when a foetus dies during an ectopic pregnancy, is too large to be reabsorbed by the body, and calcifies

At Roane Head

roane: anglicisation of *ròn* (Gaelic) meaning 'seal'

quicken: the rowan

hirpling: hobbling

the showing marks: the witch-marks, signs of enchantment

smoor the fire: to damp down the domestic fire at night, so that it smoulders till morning

scraich of day: daybreak

Beside Loch Ifrinn

Ifrinn: (Gaelic) 'Hell'; pronounced 'if-rin'

reived: removed by theft or pillage; bereft

forspoken: bewitched

skail-wind: scattering wind

scuddering: buffeting

corp-criadha: 'clay body'(Gaelic); used in witchcraft, a clay doll fashioned in the likeness of the victim was stuck through with pins to inflict pain or injury; pronounced 'corp *cree*-a'

fetch: long stretch of open water

till: stiff clay, impervious to water

libbed: castrated

score: to mark a supposed witch with a cross cut on the brow

taken: possessed; placed under a spell or curse

In Easgann Wood

stour-wind: driving storm-wind

Coille nan Easgann: (Gaelic) 'wood of the eels'; pronounced 'kul-yah nan *ess*-gen'

moon-struck: foolish

wanting a feather in the wing: simple, mentally defective

burn: stream or brook

deer-couch: flattened ground showing where deer have slept

full rank: aroused, ready for riotous behaviour

purse: pudendum

riddled: pierced

shot my roe: ejaculated

peltry: worthless rubbish; undressed skins

cullion: disagreeable person; testicle

collops: small pieces

gralloched: disembowelled

glibbed: castrated

stones: testicles

Under Beinn Ruadhainn

Beinn Ruadhainn: (Gaelic) 'summit of the red place'; pronounced 'ben roo-ah-in'; 'Ruadhainn' anglicised as 'Ruthven', pronounced 'Riven'

horn-daft: quite mad

havering: babbling, speaking nonsense

glaikit: vacant, idiotic

jilping: spurting, spilling

foosty: mouldy, gone bad

Inside Tobar nam Marbh

Tobar nam Marbh (Gaelic): 'well of the dead'; pronounced 'top-ar nam mar-uv'

thrawn: ill-tempered; twisted

querious: curious

sklent: slanted, sideways, askance

haughland: river-meadow

the simmer dim: white nights of midsummer

snow-wreaths: deep, long-lasting drifts of snow, often in corries

far ben: distant, abstracted

taibhse: (Gaelic) double; pronounced 'tie-sh', also known as swarth, co-walker, twin-brother, double-man, doppelgänger, double-ganger, fetch

the two sights: the Gaelic is *dà-shealladh* – having vision of two worlds: of sense, and of spirits – commonly known as second sight

sair-sunk: embedded

dwam: daydream, trance; stupor

sea-light, waterburn: marine bioluminescence

fankled: tangled, ensnared

wearied for: longed for

Near Gleann nam Fiadh

Gleann nam Fiadh: (Gaelic) 'glen of the deer'; pronounced 'glawn nam *fee*-ah'

flane: arrow

fiadh: (Gaelic) red deer

Làirig Ruadh: (Gaelic) Red Pass; pronounced 'lar-ig *roo*-ah'

cleuch: a gorge or ravine with precipitous, rocky sides; pronounced 'clue'

redding: cleaning the intestines

guddle: a muddle, mess

creeshie: fatty, greasy

acorné, sanglant, fracted: (heraldic) horned, bleeding, broken

paunch: entrails, viscera

forwandered: strayed off course

birling: revolving rapidly, spinning around

fleet-water: water which overflows ground

Beyond the Dubh-Chladach

dubh-chladach: (Gaelic) the 'black shore' is the stretch of beach between the sea and the high-water mark, and was regarded as an asylum from all kinds of supernatural beings; pronounced 'doo *chlad*-och'

sithchean: (Gaelic) faeries; pronounced '*shee*-ih-chun'(with 'ch' as in 'loch'); also known as the 'wee folk', 'fair folk', 'peerie folk', 'grey folk', the 'noiseless ones'

stail: gathering of stale urine, for manuring, dyeing, or as a charm against faeries

mòthan: (Gaelic) trailing pearlwort; pronounced 'mo-an'

saining: rite of blessing, protecting or purification

maistir: (Gaelic) as in *stail*; pronounced 'my-shtir'

machair: (Gaelic) fertile low-lying grassy plain close to the shore; pronounced 'ma-cher' ('ch' as in 'loch')

girning: fretful, complaining; ensnared

mimmerkin: dwarfish creature

spelled: bewitched

flitters: rag, shreds, splinters

the north-dancers: the aurora borealis

Before the Donnachaidh Falls

(this *envoi* is a protection spell)

Donnachaidh: (Gaelic) Duncan; pronounced '*don*-a-chee' ('ch' as in 'loch')

garg nuair dhùisgear